Linda Brogan

BLACK CROWS

DEDICATED TO IVERN

OBERON BOOKS
LONDON

First published in 2007 by Oberon Books Ltd
521 Caledonian Road, London N7 9RH
Tel: 020 7607 3637 / Fax: 020 7607 3629
e-mail: info@oberonbooks.com
www.oberonbooks.com

A catalogue record for this book is available from the British
Library.

ISBN: 1 84002 737 1 / 978-1-84002-737-2

Cover photograph by Richard Dean
Cover design by With Relish

Characters

MARIONETTE, string-controlled puppet; British-born Jamaican, 16

QUEENIE, Marionette's mother; Jamaican born, 45

LEANORA, British-born Jamaican, 30

HAZEL, British-born Irish / Jamaican mixed race, 15

Set As few props as possible. Queenie's Kitchen is a permanently dusty, cobweb-encrusted treadle sewing-machine and stool.

Act One

SCENE 1
YOUTH CLUB

Blackstage: no light whatsoever.

Centrestage is MARIONETTE poised over an invisible pool table.

Surrounding him are deafening sounds of a youth club: table tennis; balls slamming off the wall; pool balls clicking at other pool tables; teenagers laughing and swearing.

Underscoring this is a reggae medley from 1974 – at least two minutes.

'Here I Am (Come and Take Me)' by Al Green begins to play.

Gradually the teenage voices begin to lull.

They make a circle; signified by a blue spotlight over MARIONETTE.

The voices are deadly quiet as they wait.

MARIONETTE begins to dance gracefully, the shuffle, for the entire record.

Just outside the circle, HAZEL's yellow spotlight ignites as she watches him.

HAZEL   You'll be my stain so wide I won't be able to clean you.
You'll seep into my flesh.
You'll crawl under my skin.
I'll feel you.

Every minute of every day I'll feel you.
I'll feel when you're hungry.
I'll feel when you're lost.

You're already marked.
Soon to be mine.
Not only for Sunday best.
But in my can-wear-wardrobe.

I'll wear you day in and day out.
I'll wear you morning noon and night.
There won't be time to wash you.

The crowd does not applaud but we can feel their apprec-
iation.
The reggae medley begins again.
The youth club noises return in earnest.

MARIONETTE takes his position over the invisible pool
table.
Silently HAZEL's yellow spotlight goes out.

Blackout. Silence.

SCENE 2
QUEENIE'S KITCHEN

QUEENIE operates her treadle sewing machine throughout.
Night; moonlight coming through window.

QUEENIE   What time you call this?

MARIONETTE opens the invisible fridge door.
Blue light streams out and cuts an arc on the floor.

You wan' food you get a job.
You think me sit here all night, every night
Like raasehole Rumplethinskin for me own amusement.
Catering tin a beans is all me go buy till you find
   employment.

And no bodder tell me the state a the country.
And whether me come parents' evening or not.
You think say me wan a go end up like some black crow
Who sit a doorstep with them life in tatters.
With not a woman friend let alone a man friend.
Yes, cut your eye.
When you go out that door for the last time
It's Ray who a go comfort me.
And you see the steak me buy him
That's the price, man.
The price for comfort in your old age.
You think me wan a go starve of love.
You no see the beans there.
The big tin a beans.
The catering tin a beans.
You want eat – eat the beans.
You no like what me buy – you go look your father.
Go look your father me say.
See if him have tuppence left from the bookie.
Even the dog him take him money go waste.
Even the dog him a chase.
Even a dog him a bet upon.
But you see me.
You see me and Ray.
You see the little bit him bring in from the buses.
One day me a go step pon the soil from which me
   came.
Go ahead and laugh.
Money money, stock the money and one day you
   dream come true.
You no want the beans – shut the fucking fridge.
Shut the fridge me say.
Shut the fridge.
No wonder them no want employ you.
Stupid.
Stupid from morning.

Go ahead and dance.
Watch them turn you fool.
Like your father you'll amount to nothing.
Shut the raaseclaat door.
Me can't afford no seizure inna me finger.
These fucking finger a go take me from hell to heaven.
If I stand up you see…

MARIONETTE slams the fridge door.
The fridge light goes out.
QUEENIE operates the treadle sewing machine for at least one minute.

Go look your father if you want more than beans.

Blackout. Silence.

SCENE 3
THE STREET

Night; traffic sounds on Princess Road, a main thoroughfare.
Headlamps speed up as they go through Moss Side.
1974 police car in the distance.
MARIONETTE, drenched in its blue siren light, is walking head down.
We hear sounds of his belly rumbling.
He stops to rub it.
He sits on the kerb.
The cars carry on passing him by, really speeding up when they pass the black puppet.
A red spotlight enters the stage.
MARIONETTE eventually notices.
He looks up and stares at it.

The cars stop.
LEONORA enters the red light.
She's wearing a strappy, red, 1974, good quality dress.
She holds out a patty.

LEONORA   I may not be good looking. In fact I'm ugly. The raw
born ugliness that sets you off on a path. But you see
the cut of this dress. You can't afford this dress on no
shop-keep wage. Used to look at myself in the mirror
and thing Lord God but you're ugly. But you see that
about me. You see my ability to see. Two eyes I have.
Two eyes to use. Watch them now – clear as a bell.
Ugly. But that don't stop me. That don't clear my path.
Watch me now. Straight up to it. Straight up to the
path. Straight there in front of me. I want it. It's what
I go get. Me see it me want it me get it. Clear in the
eye. I'm ugly yes. But I'm pretty all the same. Look
how she's pretty. Cos as my eyes are open so yours are
blind.

The red spotlight envelopes them both.

What me go give you boy is pretty.

LEONORA feeds MARIONETTE the patty.

Blackout. Silence.

SCENE 4
LEONORA'S BEDSIT

That night.
Candlelit, MARIONETTE and LEONORA are sat side by side
on her bed.
Silence.
LEONORA caresses his strings.

Eye contact.
LEONORA pulls him closer.
Eye contact.
He touches her hand.
Eye contact.
He caresses her cheek.
Silence.

The pink blush in the room warms.
They hold each other.

MARIONETTE makes love to LEONORA.

SCENE 5
LEONORA'S BEDSIT

The next morning; a pink, rising sun is pouring through the window.

LEONORA   The sink I washed in before is where you'll wash the breakfast things – before you wash my panties. Make sure you change the water. Iron them gusset first, moving towards the elastic. Don't leave the Belling on it eats electric – where you'll cook tea – I'll be home at six. Here's five pounds the budget for today. I don't like chicken. And I hate rice and peas. Gutter food. Buy pasta it'll tell you what to do on the back. Pasta and mince meat. Spaghetti Bolognese. I don't drink. I don't smoke. Prepare the bed for tonight. If last night's anything to go by we'll get on like a house on fire.

LEONORA leaves.

Blackout. Silence.

SCENE 6
YOUTH CLUB

Twilight.

Centrestage is MARIONETTE poised over an invisible pool table.

Surrounding him are deafening sounds of a youth club: table tennis; balls slamming off the wall; pool balls clicking at other pool tables; teenagers laughing and swearing.

Underscoring this is a reggae medley from 1974 – at least two minutes.

'Here I Am (Come and Take Me)' by Al Green begins to play.

Gradually the teenage voices begin to lull.

The voices make a circle; signified by a blue spotlight over MARIONETTE.

The voices are deadly quiet as they wait.

Inside the blue spotlight MARIONETTE begins to dance, gracefully, the shuffle.

Just outside the circle HAZEL in her yellow spotlight watches MARIONETTE dance.

The door smashes open.

Engulfed in her red spotlight LEONORA bursts in.

LEONORA   Where's the money? Where's the fucking money? Where's me fucking money? You stink of chocolate. You're not a child.

MARIONETTE strokes her knee.

What good's pool, hey? What good's pool? I pay rent.

MARIONETTE strokes her thigh.

With these silly girls all day. Dancing for these silly girls.
  You need a big woman.

MARIONETTE puts his hands between her legs.

You know what to do with a big woman.

The crowd does not applaud but we can feel their appreciation.
The reggae medley begins again.
The youth club noises return in earnest.

MARIONETTE takes his position over the invisible pool table.
HAZEL's yellow spotlight remains.

Blackout. Silence.

SCENE 7
HAZEL'S MUM'S KITCHEN

HAZEL   Mum, move your legs and let me get the milk.
         Mum…
         Mum, move over – move out of the way of the fridge.
         Let me get some plain milk:
         Stera's fucking terrible on your cornflakes.

         It's not my fault he doesn't give you any money.

         You get fucking family allowance for me.
         No; but you do for the next month.
         Till June – till I'm sixteen.

         I'm putting them in the bin then.

         Well let us get the plain.

         Mum, just give us the plain milk.

You get family allowance for me.

You get family allowance for me.
They give it you for me.

I know you fucking spend it on me.

I can't fucking eat 'em with Stera on.

Right I'm getting your purse.

I'm only taking the money for the plain milk.

No I didn't.

You did it yourself.

No I didn't.

Mum I didn't.

It won't bruise.
I didn't mean it.

Tell me dad what you like.

All he'll say is go up the stairs.
'You no hear me go up the stairs.'
And I will.

No I don't.
I'm hardly ever here.

Are you gonna give me the plain milk or not?

Fucking stick it then.

As long as you get family allowance for me I'm staying.

You're just as bad.

You're every bit as bad.

I'm not going till I've done me O Levels – I'm going to
    university.
One month, one fucking month and then I'm out of
    here.

Mum, move away from the fridge.
Mum, lean over the sink.
Lean over the sink.
Mum, lean over the sink.
If you don't lean over the sink…
Lean over the sink.
Please.
Will you lean over the sink.
Take your glasses off.
Take your glasses off.
Take your glasses off before…
Let me take your glasses off.
Look. Look there. LOOK THERE NOW.

Sit up or you'll choke.
MUM, sit up.
Will you sit up.
Where's your knickers?
Where's your fucking knickers?
I can see all your…

SIT UP.
Fuck you then.
You stupid old cunt.
FUCK YOU THEN.
You drunken old…

It's alright – it's alright – we'll clean it up.

It takes HAZEL *ages to mop up the bucket-loads of sick.*

Blackout. Silence.

SCENE 8
QUEENIE'S KITCHEN

QUEENIE operates her treadle sewing machine throughout.
Day; sunlight is coming through the kitchen window.

QUEENIE   I hear say you shack up with she.
A thirty year-old woman.
Mind you what kind a woman is she.
A boy of sixteen.

MARIONETTE opens the fridge door.
The light cuts an arc on the floor.

Only beans did there.
But you must eat well now.
What's that you a drop?
Steak.
She must have money to waste.
Thank you.
Me nah say me nah grateful.
There'll be a price to pay.
Any woman so desperate to molest a child can't be good
   woman that.
A syndrome you see, sah, a syndrome from back home.
You nah want sit there pon your porch dressed from
   head to toe.
Black.
Black, man.
It seep in the sun and drench in the rain.
So my mumma stay from the grave open up and
   swallow your grandfather.
A sit there pon her porch a weep.
It's the living you should weep for.
New clothes she buy you too, hee.
You look like man.

Big man.
Mind you, so it go – a big woman will cast a big man.
Buckfast.
For me joints.
You're thoughtful hee.
You tell her your mumma says she's a good woman.
Breast milk – so lions stay – one can't feed – next one
    say come – me is young – full ripe breast, see it here
    so.

MARIONETTE closes the fridge.
The treadle sewing machine continues for one minute.

Blackout. Silence.

SCENE 9
YOUTH CLUB

Twilight.
*Centrestage, MARIONETTE is poised over an invisible pool
table about to take a shot.*
*Surrounding him are deafening sounds of a youth club: table
tennis; balls slamming off the wall; pool balls clicking at other
pool tables; teenagers laughing and swearing.*
*Underscoring this is a reggae medley from 1974. At least
two minutes.*

*'Here I Am (Come and Take Me)' by Al Green begins to
play.*
Gradually the teenage voices begin to lull.
*The voices make a circle; signified by a blue spotlight over
MARIONETTE.*
The voices are deadly quiet as they wait.
*MARIONETTE begins to dance gracefully, the shuffle, for the
entire record.*

Just outside the circle, HAZEL in her yellow spotlight is watching MARIONETTE dance.

Café doorbell tinkles; LEONORA enters.

LEONORA   George give me two pattie and two Cokes – one to go.
           I've put yours on the table behind you, lover. Reach
             home by ten.

LEONORA leaves.

HAZEL   Come Caz's dance.
         We're all going at midnight.

The crowd does not applaud but we can feel their appreciation.
The reggae medley begins again.
The youth club noises return in earnest.

SCENE 10
CAZ'S SHABEEN

The nearby church bell strikes midnight.
MARIONETTE and HAZEL walk side by side not talking to each other.
But every so often she looks at him or he looks at her.
They enter the seedy, dark, basement club.
Real dub reggae is thumping out of huge invisible speakers.
The sound of bottles and glasses and general patois conversation underneath.

HAZEL   I know you're staring at me.
         Not staring – looking at me.
         Watching me.

'I'm Still Waiting' by Dennis Brown begins to play.

Engulfed in her yellow spotlight HAZEL *walks towards him.*

MARIONETTE's *blue spotlight ignites.*

They meet.

There's a clap of thunder.

There's a streak of lightning.

Their merged spotlights becomes a single green spotlight.

Others part on the slippy floor.

As your arm goes round my back, I know.

I know for the first time what was between my mum
  and dad.

What all the fuss was about.

Electric.

Lightning.

Thunder.

Life.

I fit.

We fit.

Instant ignite.

Instant ignition.

My pants are wet.

I know you feel it too.

I don't have to ask – I know.

MARIONETTE *and* HAZEL *dance plastered together for the
entire record.*

I've nowhere to go.

You've nowhere to go.

The record is fading.

Into a whisper.

Like an echo.

The leaves in the park are rustling in the breeze.

A full yellow moon above them lights the silvery blue pond at their feet.

You'll have to kick open the park toilets.

Beside the pond, under the branches of the willow tree, MARIONETTE makes love to HAZEL.
Blackout. Silence.

SCENE 11
QUEENIE'S KITCHEN

Same night; early hours.
MARIONETTE sneaks HAZEL through the back door into the kitchen.
He opens the invisible fridge door.
Blue light streams out cutting an arc on the floor.

Suddenly the back door is being banged down like the street is on fire.
MARIONETTE and HAZEL freeze.
Doing up her housecoat QUEENIE is coming downstairs to open it.

QUEENIE Go back up, Ray – go back up.

QUEENIE opens the back door.
LEONORA is engulfed in her red spotlight.

LEONORA No matter which house I knock on I can't find him.

QUEENIE It's six o'clock in the morning. He's not here. Like I told you at four o'clock, at two o'clock, at midnight. Don't bother knock this door again tonight or me and you will fall out. When his pocket run dry he'll be back.

But it's not then you give in. It's not then so. You wait
him out. You have no pickney. Ain't no reason to let
him in. You keep him at arm's length and you watch
him shrivel.

LEONORA   You know. Like me you know. If they fly in your face
– if they don't watch the clock – if they think they can
do anything they like then they will. That's what he'll
do. He can't go past daylight. I have to find him.

QUEENIE   The sun is coming up.

QUEENIE shuts the back door.

Shut the fridge.
If she want eat take her home.
See if her poppa will open the door same way to you.
You nah know black man yet.
You think it accident her mumma's white.
See if it bacon sandwich him give you.

Home you take yourself.
Home to where you come from.
Cos you know same as me he wants his grandpickney
Lighter than you, let alone himself.

I've heard nothing but stories already.
Nasty little bitch.
Walking round with your head in the air like you're
    somebody.
And the whole a the place ripe with gossip about you.
How your poppa have to send you home how you're
    bad.
Legs wide open.
The whole a the neighbourhood man.
And your poppa a nice fella.
A nice upstanding man.

Close the fridge.

You think love a go sustain you.

A so you think?

Let me tell you suttem…

You see my mumma…

You see my mumma there…

Twenty-how-much years she there a sit in black.

From head to toe – from ankle to waist – from back to
   front.

Like a John Crow she used sit waiting…

Me nah know what she a wait for – except death.

Like a vulture she prayed on the living.

Suck you dry – bend your knees – cripple your back.

And fi what.

Close the fridge.

Close the fridge me say.

Just like her all you know fi do is drain.

Love – only eeedjit believe in love.

Ray – it's not love me feel – but control.

You take your sense and you take control.

You see a person's true worth.

You watch, you look, you listen.

When them in the ground what love can do you.

Life must go on you hear sah.

You have to protect and survive.

This little half-breed might be pretty

– But she no wallet, she no food, she no sustenance.

The dark skinned favour horse, yes – but that's what
   gives you control.

Prettiness put him inna him grave and her inna her
   black.

Pretty you don't want.

MARIONETTE slams the fridge.

MARIONETTE leaves through the back door.

HAZEL follows.

HAZEL   She looks like a fucking lizard.
          Black women and their furniture.
          Thick with dust – covered in cobwebs – nowhere's seen
          a brush in a month of Sundays. The net curtains are
          filthy – you can hardly see out of the window. The first
          thing me mam would say.

Blackout. Silence.

SCENE 12
HAZEL'S MUM'S KITCHEN

Later the same morning.

HAZEL   I'm not telling you again.
          I want me family allowance.

          I want it now.

          I haven't got time to fucking argue with yer – he's
          waiting for me.

          I'll get a job.

          I don't give a fuck what me dad'll say – he doesn't give
          a fuck about me.

          If I'm a whore don't you think that has something to do
          with you
          If the whole of the area has been through me don't you
          think that has something to do with you Don't you
          think that you being a loud-mouthed drunk with no
          life of her own with no social skills with no hope has
          me do what I do, has something to do with you

Oh shut up – I'm going, aren't I – you're like a stuck
   record
I don't want to sleep in your fucking beds.
On the sheets your *children* sleep on.

You're right I'm nothing to do with them anymore.
I'm not like my brother or sisters.
You seen to that.
The first time you threw me out.
You seen to that.
They weren't allowed to talk to me on the street.
They ran across the road when they seen me coming.

You can't stop me dad loving me though – can yer – yer
   dirty white bitch.

Stick it up your arse.
FUCKING STICK IT UP YOUR ARSE.

I'm lending me dad's suitcase – I'll bring it back.

Blackout. Silence.

SCENE 13

Later the same morning.
Sat in bed, LEONORA is waiting.
MARIONETTE comes home.

Silence.
He's on his knees.
She won't look at him.
He touches her arm.
She can't look at him.
He cuddles into her.

The pink blush of the room warms.
She pulls him closer.
Silence.

They hold each other.

MARIONETTE makes love to LEONORA.

SCENE 14
LEONORA'S BEDSIT

Later; the pink warmth of afternoon is flooding through the window.
LEONORA's still in bed.
MARIONETTE is getting up.

LEONORA   We're having gammon, eggs, fresh tomatoes, freshly
     squeezed orange juice, and unsliced crusty bread with
     Lurpak. When you've finished in the bath don't come
     in till I tell you.

MARIONETTE's on his way to the bathroom.

     Till I shout you. Right. Don't come in do you hear me?
     You should bring your records and record player.
     D'you want your gammon charred or done properly?
     I've always wanted white towelling robes. I knew you
     were there. I fucking knew you were there. And why
     the fuck you take any notice of her. Tonight we'll get
     your record player and move you in proper.
     You don't know how glad I was when you knocked on
     the door.

Blackout. Silence.

SCENE 15
YOUTH CLUB

Twilight.
HAZEL waits in the café – her huge suitcase is beside her.
Surrounding her are teenagers laughing and swearing.
Underscoring this is a reggae medley from 1974 – at least
two minutes.

LEONORA and MARIONETTE come in all loved up.
MARIONETTE goes straight to the pool table.
LEONORA goes straight to the counter.
Gradually the teenage voices begin to lull.

LEONORA   George give me two patties and two Cokes.

MARIONETTE stares at HAZEL; her yellow spotlight ignites.
HAZEL stares back at MARIONETTE; his blue spotlight
ignites.
LEONORA turns round.

D'you want Coke or Lilt?

The teenage voices are deadly quiet as they wait for the penny
to drop.

You nasty little half-breed bitch.

LEONORA's red spotlight ignites as she flies at HAZEL.
The teenagers make a circle, signified by a blue spotlight over
LEONORA and HAZEL.
Inside the blue light they begin to fight.

By the pool table, MARIONETTE watches.

HAZEL   He's marked.
Mine.

LEONORA Drank my champagne, ate my gammon, lay down in
               my bed. Tell her.

HAZEL   Not only for Sunday best.
               But in my can-wear-wardrobe.

LEONORA Washed my dishes, swept my floor, ironed my knickers.
               Tell her.

HAZEL   I'll wear him day in and day out.
               I'll wear him morning noon and night.

LEONORA That bastard fucked me. Tell her. That bastard fucked me.

HAZEL   He could fuck you in front of me.
               It's not what you do.
               It's not what you say.
               It's what you feel.
               And I know he feels the same.

LEONORA Had my legs over me head. Tell her. Tell her how you
               fucked me.

HAZEL   HE'S SIXTEEN AND YOU'RE THIRTY.

Slowly LEONORA walks into the oncoming car headlamps.
*MARIONETTE pushes HAZEL away from the door, runs into
the road and grabs LEONORA.*
*In the lavender sunset MARIONETTE sits LEONORA on the
kerb.*

LEONORA Take the keys. Please.

*The crowd does not applaud but we feel their appreciation.
Through the door of the cafe the reggae medley begins again.
The café noises return in earnest.*

HAZEL watches MARIONETTE lead LEONORA away.

Blackout. Silence.

SCENE 16
HAZEL'S LODGING HOUSE

Same evening.
HAZEL carrying her dad's suitcase opens the door to the empty room.
The stale, sweaty smell of other people is overpowering.
Gingerly she pulls back the filthy curtains to peek out the dirty window.

HAZEL   What the fuck have I done?

Disembodied footsteps walk along the bare corridor and shut their doors.
HAZEL can't find a lock or key on hers.
She pushes her suitcase to the door and sits on it listening to the footsteps...

What the fuck have I done?

...until she hears MARIONETTE's moccasins coming along the bare floorboard landing.
Her yellow spotlight ignites; HAZEL is up opening the door before he knocks.

I knew you'd come.
I knew I didn't imagine it.

MARIONETTE brings his record player and his box of records in.
He sets it up as HAZEL waits, sitting on her case.
He puts on 'I'm Still Waiting' by Dennis Brown.

Like a glistening bubble, the empty room erupts in translucent green fairy lights.
They dance.

Under the filthy curtains, at the dirty window, MARIONETTE
makes love to HAZEL.

Blackout. Silence.

SCENE 17
QUEENIE'S KITCHEN

The next morning.

QUEENIE   Place it pon the bottom rung a the fridge, later me braise
it for Ray if me so much as get the chance.

LEONORA   He hasn't been home all night.

LEONORA opens the invisible fridge door.
Blue light streams out and cuts an arc on the floor.

QUEENIE   Me head no sooner off the pillow. Then me hear it.
Rat a tat tat. Rat a tat tat. That's how it began. Then
bang. Bang. Bang. I looked out the window first. She
was hardly able to stand. One nasty little fat white
woman nah so high. Her two feet buckled beneath
her. And a knife in her hand. I just laugh. Ray sat
up. Lie down I told him. Lie your backside down. I
put on me housecoat. And did all the buttons. Shut
your cleat I said to him. There's a way to deal with
this type a person. Hear the doorbell. Only now she
find it. The whole a the street out pon them doorstep
when me reach the front door. Come in me tell her.
But she won't come in. Battle already won. And she
start just how I expect. 'That mongrel you reared has
my daughter.' Him nah mongrel me say to her. Him
pedigree. But me keep me voice low and lean. 'That
no good...' Yes him no good me tell her. Come in and
have a cup a tea. Me take the knife cos she's surprised

now. Yes him no good just like him farder. She happy
now because me know her and she know me. Is coffee
you want or tea? 'I don't touch…' Me neither. And
me make a whole pot because she don't look like she
sleep a drop. I know I know; I kept saying to her cos
I do. We do know. Yes it's sweet as orange blossom to
begin with but it soon sour and when it sour it can't
retrieve. Lost and strangled with him she is. Proud I'm
proud of my escape. And she look at me with renewed
vengeance. But me just laugh.

LEONORA   Is his record player still here?

QUEENIE   Soon the little half-breed back in the master's bed. You
see that is what is wrong with the mumma. Him no
longer find her attractive. Instead him have him eye on
the daughter. But you see that kind of upstanding man
would never do that. But him still send out him wife
like a tracker dog.

LEONORA   My father fucked me from the age of seven till eleven he
did seven years for it.

QUEENIE takes a bottle from the fridge.
The blue fridge-light cuts an arc on the floor.

QUEENIE   Rum punch.
Keep it chilled.
Chase the wind from your head.

Blackout. Silence.

SCENE 18
THE BOOKIE'S

Centrestage, MARIONETTE is poised under the blue light of an invisible telly above his head.
Surrounding him are the deafening sounds of the bookie's; Jamaican men placing bets.
Underscoring this is the racing commentator – at least two minutes.

Under starter's orders.
Gradually the male voices begin to lull.
They make a circle under the telly signified by a blue spotlight over MARIONETTE.
The voices are deadly quiet as they wait.
They're off – inside the blue light MARIONETTE begins to ride his imaginary horse.
He rides gracefully, to the end of the race.

Just outside the circle, HAZEL, in her yellow spotlight, watches MARIONETTE ride.

The Jamaican men whistle and slap their fingers.
The commentator begins again.
The gambling noises return in earnest.

MARIONETTE takes his position under the invisible telly.

Black out. Silence.

End of Act One.

Act Two

SCENE 1
QUEENIE'S KITCHEN

Night; moonlight coming through the kitchen window.
QUEENIE is operating her sewing machine.
MARIONETTE opens the fridge.
The blue light cuts an arc across the floor.

QUEENIE   The dark one pregnant.
The other fool a sport ring.

Marriage is not for nutten.
My mumma, and a better looking woman in white
    dress, you never seen.
Him a die and her stood there with her posy.
From white to black the next morning.
Did him leave her a penny?
Not in your raaase.
Lef it to the bitch over in Ginger Hill.
Her one there proud with her little victory.
'It's me him marry.'
Him marry her alright – with a wound.
A so you go end up.
You see that steak you're putting in there so…
And tell her me grateful…
Any choice to be made – you put that on one side of the
    scale.
It's like me talking to a piece a wood.
Me made one mistake with your father.
You see that man upstairs – him wage packet
– him wage packet every week.

43

Them want pay for you to fuck them – then fuck them
    good style.
Take what you can from the pretty one before she
    pregnant too.
Marry the ugly one.
We all ugly in the end.

SCENE 2
THE SUPERMARKET

*HAZEL engulfed in her yellow spotlight is carrying a shopping
basket.*
LEONORA engulfed in her red spotlight bursts in.

LEONORA   He's mine.

HAZEL   Is he fuck.

LEONORA   He's mine.

HAZEL   Get to fuck.

LEONORA   Where was he Friday night?

HAZEL   In the gambling house.

LEONORA   All night?

HAZEL   All night.

LEONORA   In my bed.

HAZEL   You old cunt.

LEONORA   In my bed.

HAZEL   For his dinner.

LEONORA   And that's the kind of man you want?

HAZEL   Tell your mates to back off.

LEONORA   You tell 'em.

HAZEL   Tell your mates...

LEONORA   I'm telling you...

HAZEL   Tell your fucking mates to back off.
          Hey, you at the fucking till, call the police.

LEONORA   Call any one you like, next time...

HAZEL   Call the fucking police.

LEONORA   Next time I won't buck you up, you won't hear me, you
          won't see me.

HAZEL   Why, you gonna jump under that fucking bus.

LEONORA   Little half-breed...
          My man that – bought and paid for

HAZEL   Yeah.
          The ten pound you gave him bought us lunch.
          Let go of me hair.
          Let go of me fucking hair.

          *Their combined spotlights engulf them in a burning orange
          spotlight.*

LEONORA   You might work in an office, bitch
          But you ain't got no class.
          Because you see your mother before you.
          White women man, all man tief.
          What can be expected from the mixed up daughter?
          Today me go in peace – next time...
          Pretty you pretty yes, but let's see what he thinks when
          you're nah pretty.
          You understand me?

HAZEL   If your fucking mate boots me once more…

LEONORA   Kick her, Carol.
          Save her face.
          Me want him say he come back of his own accord.

SCENE 3
HAZEL'S BEDSIT

HAZEL is putting the shopping away in the bedroom cupboard.

HAZEL   I bought us Coco Pops and coffee. I put the bet on. Two-twenty at Chepstow. Stopped it at ten to one. And paid tax. I couldn't work out how to do the accumulator. Did you ring work for me? I'll go back on Monday.

          Don't go out. I thought we were staying in bed. I put the bet on. You promised we'd spend the afternoon in bed. I put on the bet that you asked me…

          Don't go out.

          MARIONETTE slams the front door.

SCENE 4
THE SUPERMARKET

HAZEL engulfed in her yellow spotlight is carrying a shopping basket.
LEONORA engulfed in her red spotlight sweeps in.

LEONORA   She doesn't even know what an accumulator is.

HAZEL   Back your friends off.

LEONORA   Cost him how many pounds.

HAZEL   Back off.
Back fucking off.

LEONORA   Doesn't even know what an accumulator is.
But she knows how to suck cock.
She sucks cock – don't you, you dirty little bitch.
We don't suck cock.
You don't suck cock.
She don't suck cock.
None of us suck cock.
But you, you dirty bitch.

HAZEL   No wonder he don't stay there then.
Lift your leg to kick me and I'll kill yer.
Big grown women following this fool.

LEONORA   They're nasty – white women and them pickney are
nasty you see.

HAZEL   Bessies are wooden in bed.

LEONORA   Ah so you think.
Hold her.

Their combined spotlights make a burning orange spotlight.

What did I tell you?
Hey?
What did I tell you?

HAZEL   Not me face.

LEONORA   Either you leave – you leave Manchester – or me kill
you.
In my language it's one man, one woman, one child.

SCENE 5
ACCIDENT AND EMERGENCY

A nurse telling other patients which room to go to throughout.
Faint sound of ambulances in the background.
MARIONETTE and HAZEL are sat in the waiting room.

HAZEL   Who's she pregnant to? To that bloke she's been
hanging around with. To that soldier. Is she pregnant
to the soldier? Will you answer me? She'll marry him
then won't she? She can move to Kent with him.

When they've stitched me lip – they're gonna send me
dental department to do me teeth.

SCENE 6
HAZEL'S MAM'S

The sound of a Guinness being opened.
Then poured.
Then it being drunk.
At intervals throughout.

HAZEL   What do you see in me dad?

You can't tell.
They look as good as me own.
They're permanent.
They filed me teeth down.
They're on stumps.
Both front ones.

What do you see in me dad?

At least he can read and write.

He didn't miss me when I was here.

What do you see in me dad?

They're taking them out on Monday – I'm to see the
  nurse.

What the fuck do you see in me dad?

Four on the outside of me lip.
Six on the inside.
Me teeth stuck in it.

Oh you would though wouldn't yer.
Yeah, you'd box everyone down.

I got a sick note.
No I haven't been taking loads of time off work.

I ain't coming back.

I have cup-a-soups cos I like them.

No he doesn't take me money.

He can do what he likes to her I don't give a fuck.

She's pregnant to a soldier.

It fucking isn't his.

I'm the talk of the neighbourhood.
What about you?
What about you and your fucking Guinness and your
  knife in your bag.

She's not gonna attack you.

You're lying.

When?

On Princess Road?
When did this happen?

Mum, stay away from her – she's a savage black cunt.

SCENE 7
THE SUPERMARKET

LEONORA is carrying a shopping basket.
HAZEL engulfed in her yellow spotlight bursts in.

HAZEL   Stay away from me mam.

LEONORA   He's bought it a pram.

HAZEL   You bought it with your six hundred and ninety-five
          pounds' maternity benefit.

LEONORA   Like you bought the engagement ring.

HAZEL   He bought it from Samuel's.

LEONORA   Like I said.
          Twenty-two pound fifty.

HAZEL   He cracked you when you spent the big cheque on that
          thing in your belly.

LEONORA   He ain't never laid a hand on me.
          No one's seen him lay a hand on me.
          He knows you're worthless.
          In the long run worthless.
          Them kick you out of your job – hee.
          Too much time off.
          You don't get him yet do you.
          He'll wash your dish, he'll sweep your floor, he'll iron
          your knickers.

He won't earn a penny and if he won't who must.
Your day is numbered, gal, your day is numbered.

SCENE 8
QUEENIE'S KITCHEN

Night; moonlight coming through the kitchen window.
QUEENIE's operating her sewing machine.

MARIONETTE opens the fridge.
The blue light cuts an arc across the floor.

QUEENIE   They should tear you off the street and castrate you.
With two thousand brother and sisters you nah know,
   you choose to populate the world same way.
Me never thought me would say it but me look at you
   and me hate you. That this body could give birth to
   such a…
Words fail me.
Words fail me.
Two pickney on the way, two raaseclaat pickney.
Take what you want – all me hope is it choke you.

MARIONETTE shuts the fridge.

You bastard.
You bastard unnu.

QUEENIE leaves.

End of Act Two.

Act Three

THE BOOKIE'S

Centrestage, MARIONETTE is poised under the blue light of an invisible telly above his head.
Surrounding him are the deafening sounds of the bookie's; Jamaican men placing bets.
Underscoring this is the racing commentator – at least two minutes.

Under starter's orders.
Gradually the male voices begin to lull.
They make a circle under the telly signified by a blue spotlight over MARIONETTE.
The voices are deadly quiet as they wait.
They're off – inside the blue light MARIONETTE begins to ride his imaginary horse.
He rides frantically to the end of the race.

The Jamaican men moan.
The commentator begins again.
The gambling noises return in earnest.

MARIONETTE takes his position under the invisible telly.

Under starter's orders.
They're off – under the telly light MARIONETTE watches frantically to the end of the race.

The Jamaican men whistle and slap their fingers.
The commentator begins again.
The gambling noises return in earnest.

MARIONETTE takes his position under the invisible telly.

Under starter's orders.
They're off – under the telly light MARIONETTE watches frantically to the end of the race.

The Jamaican men moan.
The commentator begins again.
The gambling noises return in earnest.

MARIONETTE takes his position under the invisible telly.

Throughout, the sound of the bookie's is building.
Throughout, LEONORA's red spotlight is gradually swelling.
Throughout, HAZEL's yellow spotlight is gradually fading.

LEONORA'S BEDSIT

LEONORA I ain't got any money.
I ain't got any money left.
And the rent money you took may God forgive you.

MARIONETTE slams the front door.

HAZEL'S BEDSIT

HAZEL I haven't got any cheques left to bounce.

MARIONETTE slams the front door.

LEONORA'S BEDSIT

LEONORA I'm not giving you fifty p.
Fifty p.
You make me laugh.

You're gonna stand up in the bookie's and bet fifty p.
No probably you're gonna do ten pence each way.
Fifty p could buy a dummy.
Fifty p can buy me a pint a milk for a cup a tea.
But I don't deserve a cup a tea, do I.

MARIONETTE slams the front door.

HAZEL'S BEDSIT

HAZEL   I nearly fucking died when the old guy downstairs seen
     his envelope in me hand.
Thirty-three quid.
The guy in the post office asked for ID but I smiled at
     him.
You know that smile.
I've only spent ten pounds of it.

MARIONETTE slams the front door.

LEONORA'S BEDSIT

LEONORA   Fifty p
Rain or shine him there a bookie.
Bookie, bookie, bookie
Till your skin grey.
Watch you stand there.
Let me let you into a little secret.
You can't love.
You can't be loved.
Like ice.
Like wood.
And same you stay from morning.
From little.
Because you're dead behind the eyes.

See it there.

Go long let the bookie's draw you by the nose.

MARIONETTE slams the front door.

HAZEL'S FLAT

HAZEL   Fifty p.

In case you're interested me mam posted bail in court.

Yesterday you were winning sixty-five quid – not
   tuppence.

Sixty-five quid.

Ten minutes till the place shut and you blew it.

You blew sixty-five quid on one horse.

On one horse.

Sixty-five quid.

Two hundred pounds arrears.

But when they throw me out I'm going straight round to
   hers.

She'll put me up.

She can put me up.

Then you won't have to travel from A to B.

She can put me up then your kids can be together.

I can even use her leftover walker and bouncy chair.

That'll save a few bob.

That's what you must have had in mind when blew
   sixty-five quid.

You can sleep between us.

Turn over in rotation – one night on, one night off.

Put me purse down.

Put me fucking purse down.

I ain't giving you fifty p and if you lay a hand on me
   you see the police

They'll lock your black arse up.

Move in with her.
I don't give a fuck anymore.
In fact I'll help you move.
Put your rags in the carrier bags you brought them in.
I don't give a fuck.
D'you think I give a fuck.
Do you really think I give a fuck.
Stuck here in this flat.
Me dad don't talk to me. I can't even enter his house.
  Me little brother got sick of coming here watching how
  his sister lives. How do you think that sits with me.
  Begging me to come home while there was still time. I
  took me rent and handed it you. I even smoke roll-ups
  and look at you with cigs.
And when this thing's born…
Where you going?

Don't leave.

MARIONETTE slams the front door.
HAZEL's yellow spotlight is a glimmer.
She picks up the large cider and the bottle of pills.

LEONORA'S BEDSIT

LEONORA is ironing her hospital trousseau.

LEONORA   Raise your hand all you like.
             See me purse there.
             You'll have to drag me through the streets screaming
               and let all the people who think you're such a nice
               bloke. All the old ladies you help upstairs with their
               shopping. All the old blokes you take my money buy
               pint for. All the pickney you kick ball with. Drag me
               through the streets make them see who you are.

LEONORA's red spotlight ignites.

 Leave the purse
Leave the purse where it there.
That's the last me have, give me the fucking money.
Give me the fucking money.
Give me me fucking money.
That's the last fucking ten pound to me name.
You want me burn you with this.
I'll burn the fucking eyes out your head.

MARIONETTE pushes the iron.
He sticks it to her breast.
It sizzles through her dress.
Into her flesh.
As a pool of wee escapes her.

Blackout. Silence.

End of Act three.

Act Four

SCENE 1
HAZEL'S MUM'S KITCHEN

HAZEL I'm gonna be someone me mam. Not the mistress of
some low down black. What chance does he have?
With me O Levels...with me O Level results I can get
a good job. With me own desk and me own stapler
and me own calculator. And new friends. White
friends. The kind of friends I should have.

It'll be back to us watching telly... You on your side of
the fire. Him on his. Me in the middle on the sofa. The
three of us.

This is valuable, mum. It's now or never. I don't even
think of him.

I'm gonna get a car, mum.

Okay, okay.
Don't bang your chin down.
Hold your head up.
Let me hold your head up.
Don't just let your head go.
Jesus – remember what happened last time.

With the iron.

On her breast.

That's it now, mum.

On remand.

Yeah remand.

He'll get time.
I'm glad.
Once the psychologist approves the abortion I'll get my
   life back on track.

I best go: before me dad gets in from work

Blackout. Silence.

SCENE 2
PRISON

LEONORA   I brought you patties, and cigs.
          And chicken from your mum.
          In a basket with your name on.
          You don't have to eat the shit in here till you've been
             sentenced.

          We've made it like you live at your mum's for the
             probation reports. She's put your bed back in and I've
             taken round some of your clothes.

          I got the most beautiful real pitch pine kitchen table, for
             the three of us to eat around; believe it or not from a
             secondhand shop – I stripped it on the balcony meself
             and waxed it. And a Cannon cooker. Imagine what
             you'll be able to do on four rings.

          I've put the brass bed under the window. With the white
             wardrobe suite on the righthand side as you go in. And
             the Moses basket between them. You'll like it.

          The living room's not much cop – a bit square. But we
             can make it look like it's got a fireplace. Not one of
             them stupid electric things. If you build up the middle

– picture it. Look straight at that wall. Right. Now imagine it – say like shelves in the middle. Floor to ceiling. Then either side about a third of the way up equally distanced shelves. It'll create a chimney breast. With the cane three-piece I saw in town. And a cream shaggy rug.

I'm gonna keep it all cream. The whole flat. Cream. With floor-length cream muslin curtains. Not at the front. Not in the kitchen. I'm gonna get blinds. What d'you think. They've got this wooden pair. An arm and a leg. In the back office in work. No fucker uses it. Just there a waste. They'd look perfect. What d'you think wooden blinds at the kitchen window and the bathroom to match.

A full flat just for us. Bathroom. Kitchen. Separate bedroom with a balcony. From it the pink blossom in the park looks magnificent, man. I've planted pink sweet peas in blue pots ready for spring.

Don't let the others see you cry.

Ssssh! Wait till you see Babby. Just wait till you see her little fat legs.

MARIONETTE puts his hand out to her across the table.
LEONORA refuses it.

If she's been here... If you're taking the piss... I may have dropped the charges. But I can still turn up at court to give evidence. D'you understand me?

MARIONETTE takes her hand in his.
LEONORA blushes pink.

Blackout. Silence.

SCENE 3
LEONORA'S NEW FLAT

LEONORA is breastfeeding Babby.
There's a knock at the front door.
LEONORA puts on her cardigan to cover the dressing on her breast.
LEONORA answers the door.
LEONORA's red spotlight ignites.

HAZEL   It must be a nightmare with no lift – two floors with a pram.

LEONORA   I hear you shag white men in Genevieve's.

HAZEL   He'll have somewhere to come home to – better than your bedsit.

LEONORA   What you want?
Maybe you can't understand.
What do you want?

HAZEL   Me mam bathed me mouth when they capped the front teeth you knocked out; fetched me from the police station when I bounced the cheque; bailed me in the dock when I robbed the giro; watched them pump me stomach in the hospital; gave me a deposit so I didn't have to sleep on the fucking bloodstained mattress in the hostel. And each time when he'd had what he wanted he climbed into your nice white cotton sheets and slept.
To stop fighing with you, Leonora

LEONORA   Him there a prison and this is what you do – shag white men.

HAZEL   It's none of his business.

LEONORA   Him nah worth nothing to you?
            No matter what happens between me, you and him:
            The pickney inside you – his pickney that.

HAZEL   I want it to end now.
            Now.
            Here at this door.

            Silence.

            LEONORA's red spotlight is subsiding.

LEONORA   You look hot.
            D'you want lemonade?

HAZEL   Thank's for letting me in.

LEONORA   They've cut his hair after him grow it so high.

HAZEL   He must be well pissed off.

LEONORA   Lost his side tooth in a fight cos his head's so small.

HAZEL   Him fighting?

LEONORA   He's changed, man, he's changed.
            He's not the boy we knew.

            Silence.

            I seen your mum in the precinct – tell your mum I'm
              sorry.

            Silence.

HAZEL   A fresh start?

LEONORA   To me he comes – shoes off – for his feet rubbed.

HAZEL   It's me who's sorry.

            Silence.

LEONORA I'll get you your lemonade.

LEONORA passes HAZEL to get the lemonade.
The tip of LEONORA's fading red spotlight touches HAZEL's
weak yellow spotlight.
A mellow, Buddhist-orange light ripples where they touch.

Blackout. Silence.

SCENE 4
PRISON

QUEENIE If you didn't act like a dawg – she wouldn't need a
leash.
You've nearly rip off all me shutters to raase.

Let me tell you this – me tell you this much:
Either me leave with pictures a you in a halbum or me
leave you dead.

The whole a me a go back a success.
You settled.
The next one a naval college.
The third one as you know me a go take with me.
Leave the house round the corner lodged to the brim.
Old women wanting dresses for church.
Young women for parties.
And you see one dress – that young woman – the
mother a you pickney – at home this very minute
twisting twig into welcome banner – a go wear it for
the biggest day of her life.

Not one venom a go point them finger at me and tell me
my life ruined.

A nest you're to build – you're the other set a wings to
fly out when she a look her pickney. You'll fly from the
nest go look a worm. And then you'll fly back again
with the raaseclatt thing dangling from your mouth.
And when your chick drop it you pick it up and you
place it back whether it covered in dirt or not, because
them have to eat so the Lord God himself say. The
fruit a the trees. The worm from the soil. Cos your
pickney a go need protein. And when me left from this
place you see your little flutter flutter it will become
strong. Real stroke of your wing. You hear me. Proper
strokes like so. You fell from the nest young. Grey
nasty little feathers and your head too big. But you
see me here today. It's so you must think son. It's for
your own good. Maybe your wing did broke in the fall.
But you see in the forest I might well strength to carry
worm but me wouldn't strength to sweep you up from
the floor. Yes; me would a look over from time to time
to watch you die. Me nah leave you here to die you
hear me. Me leave you with a splint.

The day I lay down with The Vagrant.
Nobody coulda add like me.
If my mumma hadn't been penniless me would a gone
   a school.

Blackout. Silence.

SCENE 5
LEONORA'S NEW FLAT

*LEONORA's on her balcony overlooking the park, breastfeeding
the baby.*

LEONORA   Pink, Babby – pink to make the boys wink.
           The whole park full of pink.

Look at the blossom.
Listen to it sway.
Sniff.
Smell the twilight magic, Babby.
Smell the twilight magic.

End of Act Four.

Act Five

HAZEL'S NEW FLAT

Morning.

The sound of traffic.
Knocking on the front door.
HAZEL opens it
MARIONETTE, engulfed in his blue spotlight, is stood there.
HAZEL's yellow spotlight ignites.
MARIONETTE's spotlight ignites.

Silence.

HAZEL   When did you get out?

As your arm goes round my back, I know.
I know for all time what was between my mum and dad.
What all the fuss was about.
Electric.
Lightning.
Thunder.
Life.
I fit.
We fit.
Instant ignite.
Instant ignition.
My pants are wet.
I know you feel it too.
I don't have to ask – I know.

MARIONETTE enters the flat.
Their spotlights entwine.

Their combined spotlights turn green.
HAZEL leads MARIONETTE by the hand to her bed.

'I'm Still Waiting' by Dennis Brown purrs for the entire record.

Afternoon.

The sound of traffic.

There's a knock at the front door.
HAZEL and MARIONETTE, luxurious in their green spotlight,
turn over in bed.

Our room is a cherry all beautiful and round.
Where I lie in your arms all day.
And the sun through the cracks in the curtain tell us the
    time.
And the grooves in the record tell us how much we play.
Then we fuck.
Then we lie.
Then we fuck.
Then I kiss you again.

Early evening.

The sound of traffic.
Again, there is a knock at the front door.
HAZEL hands MARIONETTE his Coco Pops, putting her
finger to her lips.

Ssssh. Coco Pops.

Later in the evening.

The traffic has stopped.
There's a knock at the front door.
MARIONETTE turns the TV down.

LEONORA   I know you're in there.

HAZEL   Turn the TV off.

There's another knock at the front door.

LEONORA   I know you're in there.

LEONORA begins to pace up and down.
The footsteps are getting louder.
Echoing in HAZEL's bedroom.
Thundering in HAZEL's bedroom.
HAZEL and MARIONETTE are motionless.

Silence.

Unseen, LEONORA begins to wheel her pram up and down.
The creaking wheels are getting louder.
Echoing in HAZEL's bedroom
Thundering in HAZEL's bedroom.
HAZEL and MARIONETTE are motionless.

Silence.

The front door is being knocked again.
Knocked more urgently – echoing in HAZEL's bedroom
More urgently again – thundering in HAZEL's bedroom.
HAZEL and MARIONETTE are motionless.

Silence.

The letterbox is being lifted up and let to clatter.
Over
And over
Again.
The noise is raining down on them in the bedroom.
They're wincing from the noise.

Neighbours begin to shout in a fog of voices.

(*At neighbours.*) Fuck off.

The front door is being kicked.
The kicking is getting louder.
The neighbours are getting louder.
The noise is deafening.
The front door is threatening to give.
MARIONETTE begins to pace the room.
HAZEL sits on the bed.
The letterbox is being clattered.
The front door is being kicked.
The neighbours are shouting.
The baby starts crying.
The noise is whipping the bedroom like huge waves on the
sea.

I know you're in there.

HAZEL   Fuck off.

LEONORA   I know you're in there.

HAZEL   Fuck off.

The noise suddenly stops.

LEONORA   (*Through the letterbox.*) I know you're in there.
Where's he?

HAZEL   Fuck off.

LEONORA   I know he's in there.
I know you're in there.
I know he's fucking in there – open the door.

The letterbox clanging starts up again.
The door kicking.

The baby crying.
The pram rolling.
The neighbours.
The noise is all but shaking the room.

He's in there.
That cunt is in there.

(*Through the letterbox again.*) I know you're in there.
He's fucking in there.
That cunt is in there.
Your daddy's in there.

Silence.

The baby's cold.
Tell him the baby's cold.

Silence.

I'll kill the baby.
I'll kill the baby.
I'll chuck the baby over the side.

HAZEL   She won't.
She won't.
Don't be fucking stupid – she won't.

LEONORA   She's out of the pram.
I've her out of the pram.
I'm gonna chuck her now.

HAZEL   A neighbour'll stop her.
Don't open the door.
A neighbour will stop her.

HAZEL grabs hold of MARIONETTE's strings.

The letterbox clattering begins again.

The door kicking.
The neighbours.
The baby cries.

 See I told you.
She'll go away soon.

The door is continually knocked.
The letterbox clattered.
The door kicked.
The baby crying.
The neighbours intermittently shouting.
Other front doors and windows being intermittently opened
and slammed.
For at least a minute until it becomes a blind ache.
The front door gives way.
LEONORA bursts in like a whirlwind.
Straight into the kitchen.
The kitchen is steeped in LEONORA's red light throughout.
Straight to the kitchen cupboard.
She destroys every scrap of food.
Throws the Coco Pops in the air.
Throws the coffee granules all over them.
Throws the milk all over them.

Silence.

HAZEL and MARIONETTE go into the kitchen – it is still
red in there.

LEONORA   Four weeks up and down like an eedjit.
           Four weeks me starve while you eat like a king.
           For you to shack up with this hard faced bitch.
           Well you'll nam shit.
           Cos she ain't got no money after that lot ruin.

HAZEL   He's gonna get a job.

LEONORA   You come dip your wick same place as half of Moss
         Side.

HAZEL   I've told him already.

LEONORA   And you've nothing to say about that.
         The sheets on my bed smell a me if not you.
         And you come lie down…
         She don't even wash them, man, I can smell them from
            here.
         Put your coat on.

HAZEL   He's going nowhere.

LEONORA   Put your coat on.

HAZEL   He's with me.

LEONORA   PUT YOUR COAT ON I WON'T TELL YOU
         AGAIN.
         Move out of me way.

         LEONORA grabs hold of half of MARIONETTE's strings.
         HAZEL still has hold of hers.
         MARIONETTE is crucified.

         You can't hear your lamb a cry.

HAZEL   And what about this?

LEONORA   What about its mixed up raase?
         Is your mumma ever gonna push it through the
            precinct.
         Will your poppa leave it darken his front door.
         Me hear about them already.
         Them won't even let this fool in.
         You ever see inside her house.

No me know you never.
Why you think him fuck a white woman
– cos him own colour shame him.

HAZEL   Get out.
Before I call the police.

LEONORA   Call who the fuck you want.
He's coming with me.

HAZEL   Let go of him.

LEONORA   You fucking let go of him.

HAZEL   Let go of him.

LEONORA   I'm warning you now – let fucking go of him.

HAZEL   Think of today.
Think of what today means.
I didn't buy him a bean.

LEONORA grabs a pair of yellow kitchen scissors and cuts MARIONETTE's strings.
MARIONETTE falls onto the ruined food on the floor.
LEONORA red spotlight leaves.

HAZEL sits MARIONETTE up.
Their combined spotlight is green.
'I'm Still Waiting' by Dennis Brown hums in the background for an entire record.
The green light is fading into yellow light as the blue light and the music fades away.
HAZEL stares at the yellow sun just rising in the doorway.

The end.

Printed in the USA
CPSIA information can be obtained
at www.ICGtesting.com
LVHW020942171024
794056LV00003B/924

9 781840 027372